ONE'S
PERSPECTIVE

ONE'S
PERSPECTIVE

ONE'S PERSPECTIVE

Poetry for the Past Fifty Years
in a Singer-Songwriter Style with
a Baby-Boomer's Point of View

TIMOTHY J. DONOVAN JR.

ONE'S PERSPECTIVE
**Poetry for the Past Fifty Years in a Singer-Songwriter
Style with a Baby-Boomer's Point of View**

iUniverse books may be ordered through booksellers or by contacting:

iUniverse
1663 Liberty Drive
Bloomington, IN 47403
www.iuniverse.com
1-800-Authors (1-800-288-4677)

*Because of the dynamic nature of the Internet, any web addresses or links contained in
this book may have changed since publication and may no longer be valid. The views
expressed in this work are solely those of the author and do not necessarily reflect the
views of the publisher, and the publisher hereby disclaims any responsibility for them.*

*Any people depicted in stock imagery provided by Getty Images are models,
and such images are being used for illustrative purposes only.*
Certain stock imagery © Getty Images.

ISBN: 978-1-5320-6737-2 (sc)
ISBN: 978-1-5320-6736-5 (e)

Library of Congress Control Number: 2019901031

Print information available on the last page.

iUniverse rev. date: 01/28/2019

Dedicated to my parents:
my mother, who instilled confidence,
and my father, who gave me a voice.

Contents

Preface xi

Introduction xiii

Chapter 1:   Ideas Turned into Words 1

   • A Poem (The Process) 3
   Postscript to Chapter 1 5

Chapter 2:   One Look from Afar 7

   • At Others' Expense 9
   • You Must Win to Be a Winner 10
   • The State of Flux 11
   Postscript to Chapter 2 13

Chapter 3:   A Stronger Feeling Never Felt 15

   • Dreaded News 17
   • Our Soul Mates 18
   Postscript to Chapter 3 20

Chapter 4:   This Love of Ours Never Ends 21

   • My Lovely Little Lady 23
   • Love of a Father 24
   • Together Forever 25
   • Thoughts of You 26
   Postscript to Chapter 4 27

Chapter 5:   This Deduction Must Be Fate 29

   • The Quest 31
   • My Masterpiece Is You 34

- Life Is Worth Pursuing 36
- Postscript to Chapter 5 37

Chapter 6:   Outhouse to the Loo 39
- We Are What We Read 41
- Nothing Comes to Mind 42
- We Are What We Do 43

Postscript to Chapter 6.................................... 45

Chapter 7:   What Did We Learn That We Should Not Know?.. 47
- The Fine Line 49
- Things We Were Taught to Believe.......................50
- Wake Up, Sunshine 52
- Save Yourselves 53

Postscript to Chapter 7....................................56

Chapter 8:   Imagine a Deserted Beach 57
- My Mirror Must Be Broken.....................59
- A Place We Only Dream Of 60
- I Need a Vacation 61

Postscript to Chapter 8..63

Chapter 9:   Afraid as I, and Wishes of We 65
- Take a Moment (Just Listen) 67
- It All Seems So Futile 69
- We All Need a Little Love 70

Postscript to Chapter 9..72

Chapter 10: Never Expose Your Chin 73
- Two Digits (Triskaidekaphobia).............................75
- If It Hurts...76
- Smile 77

Postscript to Chapter 10..78

Chapter 11: You Can't Be Wrong.................................79

    • Disagreements 81
    • A Hollow Genius.................................82
    • Negotiations 83
   Postscript to Chapter 11 84

Chapter 12: Our Coincidence of Meeting....................85

    • I Want to Be There...............................87
    • Never Needed Anyone...........................89
    • How Many Times? 90
   Postscript to Chapter 12.......................................91

Chapter 13: Alleviate the Pain................................93

    • Ode to a Friend...................................95
    • Someday Soon 96
    • Chasing That Elusive Ghost 97
   Postscript to Chapter 13.......................................99

Chapter 14: For Better or for Worse.......................... 101

    • I Wonder about Her 103
    • Now and Forevermore 104
    • A Confusion Delusion (Divorce, of Course) 105
   Postscript to Chapter 14.................................... 106

Chapter 15: Nothing Forever Survives...................... 107

    • Life in a Nutshell................................ 109
    • Success.. 110
    • Life's Too Short 111
    • The Ultimate Goal 112
   Postscript to Chapter 15.................................... 113

Chapter 16: One Question...115
    • Final Thoughts (Life's Conundrum).................... 117
Postscript to Chapter 16.. 118

Closing Words 119

Preface

One's Perspective is divided into sixteen chapters. Each chapter is titled with a line from one of the poems in that chapter. An opening paragraph precedes the poems to give the reader a hint of what's to come. At the end of each chapter, following the poems, there is a postscript identifying the year each poem was written and the addition of some insight into the creation of each individual poem. This material is placed after the poems so as not to influence the reader.

Introduction

Welcome to *One's Perspective*, a collection of works I have been writing for the past fifty years—yes, from the 1960s to the present day—that speak of teenage curiosity, lost and found relationships, social turmoil, and hopefully the wisdom of the years. As we navigate our individual paths in life, we are exposed to different experiences that transform our personal points of view. As I recently read some of my early poems again, I found it fascinating, that I was compelled to write down my feelings about a given topic as if they needed to be documented for prosperity or preserved for some future book decades down the line.

A good percentage of these so-called poems started out as songs. Music has always been a big influence in my life, from the early days of hearing doo-wop sung on the street corners of the Bronx, to the British Invasion that swept the country and the days of being the lead singer of a rock band back in my teenage years. The lyrics of the songs were always important to me. They needed to be analyzed and deciphered for hidden meanings. Later came the love of poetry, the ability to paint incredible pictures in one's mind with just words on the page. I found it truly inspiring.

Now in my mid-sixties, I find myself retired after having worked forty years building sophisticated electronic hardware for the US Armed Forces and NASA space programs. I look back to see that I have been on both sides on the fence when it comes to issues about politics, religion, war, and social events. I guess most of us can say the same. If not, then your feet may be too big to walk in others' shoes. In any case, as you read each poem, you may find some of them juvenile and, may I say, others somewhat profound. I hope the experience will rekindle thoughts of a time when you may have felt the same way. Always remember though, that no matter how you feel after reading them, it is just One's Perspective.

CHAPTER 1

Ideas Turned into Words

This opening chapter contains only one contribution, "A Poem (The Process)," outlining the method by which a poem is inspired, composed, and conveyed to an intended target, searching for that ultimate connection between writer and reader.

- A Poem (The Process)

A Poem (The Process)

The Inspiration

A poem, ideas turned into words,
sparking of synapses, creating connections,
penned to promote thought, igniting imagination,
transferred from heart to mind or vice versa,
asking, "Have you experienced this too?"

The Words

It is the use of language
to provoke an emotion and cast a shadow.
And as with all forms of communication,
it should be accepted with the knowledge
that it is just one person's point of view
at that precise moment in time.

The Instant

Knowing that one's attitude and opinions
are continuously evolving, that by chance
the readers find themselves at the
exact moment in mind
that stimulated the ultimate idea and
that motivated the author to write the words.

The Link

A connection made by people
who may have never met but share a moment,
pro or con, that prompts the individual to either stop
or read on. I hope you choose the latter. Enjoy.

Postscript to Chapter 1

"A Poem (The Process)," written in 1970, arose from a high school assignment to give a speech on any topic. I choose poetry. This was my introduction.

CHAPTER 2

One Look from Afar

Sometimes our eyes see what we want them to see and not quite reality. We may find our own problem complicated but discover that it is easy to solve others' problems, which are at a distance. We may give credit to a celebrity for accomplishing nothing, but we must always be prepared to see how our surroundings are continually changing. The three poems in this chapter reflect these sentiments.

- At Others' Expense
- You Must Win to Be a Winner
- The State of Flux

At Others' Expense

A bird in a cage, wishing to be freed.
A misplaced flower considered a weed.
One held captive; the other pulled away.
Beauty's in the eye, one may say.

Release the rare tiger back in the wild.
Near an old village with a hungry child.
Then one may eat, whereas the other may not.
Survival of the fittest is all they've got.

Some people feel the need to get involved.
the problems they solve, without common sense.
It may be good for them, and it's not so hard,
but not in my backyard, it's at others' expense.

Looking at life from a different perspective
may alter your sight and change the objective.
One look from afar sees not all the views.
Your opinions matter if you walk in others' shoes.

You Must Win to Be a Winner

Exhausted, you rise to your feet, reluctantly accepting defeat.
The difference could not have been sliced thinner.
Physically you gave all you got, though you feel the others did not.
You must win to be considered a winner.

A team will venture so far when led by an arrogant star
who has individual goals to attain.
He may be applauded, worshipped, and rewarded
for being great in a losing campaign.

Successful teams come together, aiding
and supporting one another,
each one a sum of the parts.
Encouraging words will be ample as you lead by example.
Strike the beat of unison hearts.

Always strive to be the best while including all the rest.
Stay engaged in the battle you wage.
Forever know that the mission is to beat the competition,
with everyone on the same page.

So, if you have selfish intent, seek personal accomplishment,
and choose not to let others in,
then it won't be shocking news as you continue to lose
that to be a winner, you just need to win.

The State of Flux

The present now will come and be gone.
The clocks will stop while time moves on.
Boisterous voices cease. The silent one sings.
Nothing is permanent. The pendulum swings.

What is here today will be gone tomorrow.
Total bliss will replace overwhelming sorrow.
The motionless will develop their wings.
Nothing is permanent. The pendulum swings.

But someone will stand tall while another one ducks.
You, surviving on small change, will soon have big bucks.
Sometimes the wind blows, while other times it sucks.
Just the uncertainty, living in the state of flux.

Cities will be jungles; the forest will be paved.
Leaders will be followers; the free will be enslaved.
Prisoners will be jailers; peasants will be kings.
Nothing is permanent; the pendulum swings.

Presidents will falter; dictators will stumble.
Communism will fall; democracies will crumble.
All here and now will become other things.
Nothing is permanent. The pendulum swings.

But someone will stand tall while another one ducks.
You, surviving on small change, will soon have big bucks.
Sometimes the wind blows, while other times it sucks.
Just the uncertainty, living in the state of flux.

For no one knows what the future brings.
Nothing is permanent. The pendulum swings.

Postscript to Chapter 2

"At Others' Expense" was written in 2004 as a song. Don't you love the ones who decide what's best for others?

"You Must Win to Be a Winner" was written in 2005. Let's stop praising losers. Encourage, yes, but stop the practice of handing out trophies for all.

"The State of Flux," written in 2016, is poem written on a tour bus in Germany that was later turned into a song. It reflects on the idea that nothing is permanent and change is constant.

CHAPTER 3

A Stronger Feeling Never Felt

This chapter has only two poems, both of which speak of the loss of a loved one. The first addresses the unexpected news for two separate women that have contrasting reactions. The second describes experiencing the ultimate loss of the closest person to you on earth.

- Dreaded News
- Our Soul Mates

Dreaded News

Nonbeliever

She paused, then sighed,
tears she cannot hide,
a stronger feeling never felt.
With a frown, her head dropped down.
Hands together, she knelt.

"If I dare, I solemnly swear,
what must be said isn't hard.
If this is true, I have no one to turn to.
How can anyone believe in God?"

Believer

She paused, then sighed,
tears she cannot hide,
a stronger feeling never felt.
With a frown, her head dropped down.
Hands together, she knelt.

"If I dare, may I recite a prayer?
What must be said isn't hard.
If this is true, all I ask of You
is to open Your arms, almighty God."

Our Soul Mates

I went to a wake the other night.
A good friend's spouse had passed away.
My greeting was a heartfelt hug,
knowing not what to say.

The sadness filled the entire room
and radiated down the hall.
The loss of the love of your life
is the ultimate loss of all.

So many things I could have said,
but I uttered not a word.
The ideas abounded in my head.
I wish you could have heard.

I know your sorrow does run deep,
and as to your loss you question why.
Your life together you long to keep,
but our soul mates can never die.

For when we find love and unite as one,
nothing can take that away.
Our time together—the sorrow, the fun—
is with us every day.

So, whenever you want to communicate,
just talk; it doesn't matter where.
Any old time, any given date—
you know what they'd say: they're there.

The present is hard, the past was good,
and we know not what the future holds.
The sadness will turn to joy, as it should,
when memories begin to unfold.

So, grieve now, get it out,
and understand it's not all goodbye.
We may not know what it's all about,
but our soul mates can never die.

Postscript to Chapter 3

"Dreaded News," written in 1972, depicts the juxtaposition of faith amid a time of crisis. This poem was originally title "Telegram for a Newly Made Widow".

"Our Soul Mates" was a poem written in 2007, turn into a song and is about friends who lost their loved ones much too early.

CHAPTER 4

This Love of Ours Never Ends

This chapter consists of four poems of love: one about mutual love, one about the love of a father for his daughter, one about a lifelong love, and the last about a love that you just can't get out of your mind.

- My Lovely Little Lady
- Love of a Father
- Together Forever
- Thoughts of You

My Lovely Little Lady

I like to go to the beach, to take a walk on the sand.
I like to confide in someone I know will understand.
I really enjoy seeing a friend I haven't seen for a while.
And I cherish the look of a baby's smile.

I like to walk in the rain, as long as I'm prepared.
I like to make someone laugh when they're feeling sad.
I really enjoy mornings at the break of day.
How about a gorgeous sunset followed by the Milky Way?

But I love to love my lovely little lady,
and my lovely little lady loves me.
Destiny has we together forever,
as far as the eye can see.

There're so many things in the world
one can really like. They're not hard to think of.
But when you get down to it, there's so very few
things that we truly love.

I like to scream at the top of my lungs when I'm home all alone.
I like to hear my father's voice when I pick up the phone.
And the smell of fresh coffee served in a glass cup.
I like a cold, dry martini shaken, with a twist, straight up.

But I love to love my lovely little lady,
and my lovely little lady loves me.
Destiny has we together forever,
as far as the eye can see.

Love of a Father

I hope you know how much I love you
and how proud I am to know your mine.
When I look into your beautiful eyes
I can feel the sunshine.
You're everything I could ever wish for
in this wild and wonderful world.
I dreamed of someday having a child,
a precious little girl
just like you, for some lucky guy
to feel about you the same way that I do.
The first time I saw you, my life did change
in so many incredible ways.
And as you progressed throughout the years,
I enjoyed every phase.
An infant to a child, a teenager, a woman,
a mother and wife.
I recall dance recitals, sweet sixteen, your wedding—
an amazing life
led by you with your mother's love,
who feels the same way about you that I do.
And as I held your little hand,
with anticipation I watched you grow.
Please never forget, I am here for you
and plan on never letting go.
The greatest structures on earth
are held together with mere mortar.
There is no greater bond in the world than
the love of a father for his daughter.
What I wish for you is for the whole world
to feel for you the same way that I do.

Together Forever

When the end is near, it can truly be frustrating.
The mind isn't always clear; it's hard communicating.
How can I say thank you for everything you've given?
You're the one I've turned to; you made my life worth livin'.

From the mountain to the canyon, together for the ride.
My lifelong companion, always by my side.
We achieved so much together, sticking to our plan,
no matter what the weather, walking hand in hand.

If we stop and look back to see all that we've done,
it certainly is a fact that we truly did have fun.
To see our family grow from the promise that we vowed.
It only goes to show how much they've made us proud.

Spreading what we started, we share with family and friends.
Though we may be parted, this love of ours never ends.
Remember all the good things; it will surely make you smile.
Don't worry what tomorrow brings; I'm with you all the while.

Thoughts of You

I wake up every morning and roll out of bed.
I make a pot of coffee so I can clear my head.
I think of all the things that I had planned to do,
but I can't stop thinking about seeing and being with you.

It doesn't matter where I go or whomever I may see.
Life is filled with distractions, many they may be.
Although my mind can find the time to think another way,
I have thoughts of you, I do, continually through every single day.

I review the morning paper and read between the lines.
I peruse the news on TV for hints of intelligent signs.
I wonder just how much of what we hear is true.
But I can't stop thinking about seeing and being with you.

It doesn't matter where I go or whomever I may see.
Life is filled with distractions, many they may be.
Although my mind can find the time to think another way,
I have thoughts of you, I do, continually through every single day.

I leave the house, get in the car, and join the daily grind.
Before I'm gone, I turn the radio on to occupy my mind.
I can hear what they're saying and the songs they play too,
but I can't stop thinking about seeing and being with you.

It doesn't matter where I go or whomever I may see.
Life is filled with distractions, many they may be.
Although my mind can find the time to think another way,
I have thoughts of you, I do, continually through every single day.

Postscript to Chapter 4

"My Lovely Little Lady," written in 1972, is a song (a ditty) expanded on slightly in 2006.

"Love of a Father," written in 1972, was originally a love song called "Girl." I modified it in 2016 to express a father's love for his daughter.

"Together Forever," written in 2015, is a poem dedicated to my friends Craig and Jane for a lifetime of love.

"Thoughts of You," written in 2010, is a song with a very catchy chorus.

CHAPTER 5

This Deduction Must Be Fate

The three poems in this chapter focus on the chase, whether it be the hunt for the secrets to the universe, the personal pursuit of perfection, or learning how to enjoy every day. The answers are revealed.

- The Quest
- My Masterpiece Is You
- Life Is Worth Pursuing

The Quest

Investigation

I set off for the mountains in the distance.
Who knows what tomorrow may bring?
In search for someone with the answers,
The solution that solves everything.

Near nightfall at the edge of the forest
Stood a man with a long gray beard
Reciting what seemed to be foreign at first.
While I was approaching, it became perfectly clear.

There were people asking him questions.
For his response, I heard him say,
"The answer to ultimate inner peace is
haddi boddi goon don day."

Concurrence

I set sail for an isle in the ocean
While wondering what lay ahead,
Still searching for definitive answers,
Remembering what the old man said.

Dawn light shines upon the shoreline,
Illuminating a lady so fair.
Addressing the gathering of natives,
Her massage permeates the air:

"I have received the key to the kingdom,
A direction, how to live the right way.
Follow the path inside your heart. It's
haddi boddi goon don day."

Liberated

So, I set forth upon a new direction,
far from the perceptions of truth,
away from the familiar faces,
a fresh look at the innocence of youth.

To where the sun rises in the west in the morning
and sets brilliantly in the eastern sky,
where the rivers run forever somewhere
and no one ever questions why.

The answers to all of the issues
lie not in the bed where you lay
but is found in the adage or expression
"Haddi boddi goon don day."

Resolution

Now I set my mind free of any confusion.
Question not what needs to be solved.
Overwhelmed by a feeling of knowing,
That all doubt has now been dissolved.

My journey's answers have all been in common.
Everywhere I heard its praise.
Who knew that the final conclusion
would be found in a simple phrase?

So, when you find yourself in the doldrums
wondering why, know that it will be okay.
The answer lies deep down within you:
"Haddi boddi goon don day."

My Masterpiece Is You

I was busy trying to create
the best rhyme of mine to date.
I struggled, I pondered. But wait,
this deduction must be fate.

Fixated on photos on the wall,
I see my son and daughter when they were small.
Where did the time go? I try to recall.
They're everything I wished for after all.

My masterpiece is you,
not just one, but two.
There is nothing better I can do.
My masterpiece is you.

I would love to record the greatest song
with music, lyrics, and meaning strong.
And everyone would love to sing along,
though my quest for perfection is wrong.

I often dream that I may write
wonderful words one could recite,
a quotation where imagination takes flight.
But I realize now what's right.

My masterpiece is you,
Mom, and I gave the world just two.
There is nothing better I can do.
My masterpiece is you.

Sometimes we strive for things we already have,
then they seem to appear out of thin air.
Trying to get to a place that's all in your mind,
not even knowing you're already there.

In my shoes, I may choose to work forever,
develop rhymes that sometimes are clever.
But there is no dough throughout this endeavor.
It's true, the two of you: I'll do better never.

So you may decide to pick up the pieces.
Someday we'll see both Timmy's and Denise's,
our grandchildren, your nephews and nieces,
a chance to create your own masterpieces

My masterpiece is you.
There's not one, but two.
There is nothing better I can ever do.
My masterpiece is you.

Life Is Worth Pursuing

Everywhere that I go, everybody wants
to know how I am feeling.
But I believe it shows from my head to
my toes. Looks can be revealing.

It is nice to share, and the fact that one
may care about how I'm doing.
But take a look at me, then you will begin
to see that life is worth pursuing.

Absolutely, positively I'm feeling fine.
Blue sky is all I see, nothing but sunshine.
Hear the birds singing; stop and smell the roses.
Enter the gate, participate, before this opening closes.

Wherever you go, be sure to say hello.
Make someone else feel good.
It may take a while, but just a smile. You
can change a neighborhood.

Shake a hand. Try to understand, the
distance between is not so wide.
Look in their eyes. You may be surprised
to see yourself on the other side.

Metaphorically, categorically I'm doing great.
Smooth sailing is all I see. Hop aboard; don't wait.
Breathe in the positivity. Absorb as the transformation starts.
Invigorate, rejuvenate. Appreciate how negativity departs.

Postscript to Chapter 5

"The Quest" was written in 2007. "Haddi boddi goon don day" is a phrase that means nothing but represents everything. I started to say it to my kids when they were babies. It would make them laugh.

"My Masterpiece Is You" is a song I wrote in 2007 for my son and daughter, who now have their own masterpieces. This one has some of my best writing.

"Life Is Worth Pursuing," written in 2018, is a poem I changed into a song within the space of two days. I believe it is important to actively pursue positive thoughts and actions and spreading it everywhere you go.

.

CHAPTER 6

Outhouse to the Loo

There are times in a poet's life when he can overdo a single rhyme. This chapter starts and ends with this premise, though they are fun to write and to read. Whereas the second poem in this chapter speaks of nothing at all.

- We Are What We Read
- Nothing Comes to Mind
- We Are What We Do

We Are What We Read

We are what we read, the plant from the seed,
the flower to the weed, a concept to a creed.

We are what we read. Our appetites we feed.
Emotionally we bleed in fulfillment of a need.

We are what we read. Mounted on our steed,
imagination we heed, for reality we impede.

We are what we read, the silk to the tweed,
the pearl to the bead, a follower to the lead.

We are what we read. For answers we plead,
our minds to be freed. Very interesting indeed.

Nothing Comes to Mind

I feel like writing something now,
but as I dwell, I find.
Just sitting here, I don't know how
nothing comes to mind.

Shall I write of funny things
or more serious ideas?
I'm learning as each word comes,
and the next line appears.

I feel I have something to say—
what it's all about.
But I can't seem to find a way
to get my feelings out.

So, I will just change my plans,
find something else to do.
Here and now, as it stands,
I must get back to you.

We Are What We Do

We are what we do,
a captain or the crew,
an elephant to the shrew,
a cue ball to the cue.

We are what we do,
a steak or the stew,
the ingredients in the brew,
to swallow or to chew.

We are what we do,
a yawn or an achoo,
likely out of the blue.
Gesundheit or bless you.

We are what we do,
a foot to the shoe,
to nail or to glue,
outhouse to the loo.

We are what we do,
to cheer or to boo,
an owl with a coo,
or a bull with a moo.

We are what we do,
the many to the few,
the pulpit to the pew,
in a yacht or a canoe.

We are what we do,
Eskimo to igloo,
an animal in a zoo,
to sue or not to sue.

We are what we do,
the old to the new,
competent to snafu,
wondering who is who.

We are what we do,
waiting in the queue,
a count of three and two,
noticing the wind blew.

We are what we do,
seeing what we drew,
flowers covered in dew,
the shade in the hue.

We are what we do,
sowing what we grew,
the Christian and the Jew,
Buddhist to Hindu.

We are what we do,
if we only had a clue
what is false or what is true.
We wish we only knew.

Postscript to Chapter 6

"We Are What We Read" was written in 2012. I call this style repetitive rhyme time.

"Nothing Comes to Mind," written in 2013, is a poem of pure nonsense but fun.

"We Are What We Do" was written in 2015. Repetitive rhyme time again.

CHAPTER 7

What Did We Learn That We Should Not Know?

This chapter consists of four poems that speak of juvenile vulnerability, common traditions, biases, and religion and the relationship between teaching and programming.

- The Fine Line
- Things We Were Taught to Believe
- Wake Up, Sunshine
- Save Yourselves

The Fine Line

The youth are always learning
while determining who they are.
New ideas are always churning,
whether lucid or a bit bizarre.
For this is a prime time to glean
identification and association,
realize the fine line between
education and indoctrination.

Things We Were Taught to Believe

I remember when we were quite young
and the things we were taught to believe.
I was an innocent impressionable child,
to the ways of the world naive.

I recall when I lost a tooth;
the incident seemed so scary.
But was told place it under the pillow
to receive money from the tooth fairy.

It made an apprehensive child calm.
Oh, how happy it made me feel.
How disappointed was I when
I found the story wasn't real.

But soon I was comforted by a tale
of a hare that would come in the spring.
We would color eggs, and he would hide them.
Then we'd search and enjoy candy he would bring.

It made an apprehensive child calm.
Oh, how happy it made me feel.
How disappointed was I when
I found the story wasn't real.

But every winter came Santa Claus,
the decorations, and all the toys.
We would wake up to find so many gifts,
only if we were good girls and boys.

It made an apprehensive child calm.
Oh, how happy it made me feel.
How disappointed was I when
I found the story wasn't real.

So, I would end every day with a prayer,
as every child was taught to do.
I would ask for the Lord's guidance
to discern the false from the true.

It gave an adolescent child alarm.
How unhappy it made me feel.
How disappointed was I when
I realized my world was surreal.

Wake Up, Sunshine

Wake up, sunshine. Open up your eyes.
Take me to where the birds go and where the angels fly.
Come on now, sunshine, please don't turn away.
Take me to a new land, a new time, another day.

When we were just children, we enjoyed playing games.
Although we looked different, we were essentially the same.
Always treat others the way you want them to treat you,
as if he were your brother, in everything you do.

Where did the innocence go?
What did we learn that we should not know?

Now that we are all educated, we think we know so much more,
more than just juvenile thoughts, so much smarter than before.
But while we were learning, we were destined to repeat history.
Fear and distrust of each other festered in a world of hypocrisy.

Wake up, sunshine. Open up your eyes.
Take me to where the birds go and where the angels fly.
Come on now, sunshine, please don't turn away.
Take me to a new land, a new time, another day.

Save Yourselves

Each will tell you they are the chosen ones, that
they will teach you and show you the way.
Then they'll empty your pockets of your meager funds
while telling you just what to say.

It is the belief that brings us together
and the reason that tears us apart.
It is not enough to love one another.
Understanding is a dying art.

I have been to the city of Jerusalem,
where three great religions were born.
Jews, Christians, and Muslims come
to celebrate, commemorate, and mourn.

Some feel the Messiah has yet to arrive,
while others know him by name.
It's why they survive, continue to thrive.
From afar, they all are the same.

Each one will tell their own story,
that the Lord is truly their friend.
Only they will rise in his glory,
while the others will perish in the end.

I have visited Vatican City,
found wealth behind every door.
Now isn't it all such a pity, attained
on the backs of the acts of the poor.

Let's now forget the pedophile protectors,
the clergy who defended their own,
by sending those offending to other sectors,
just praying, clearly saying they condone.

Now what about the evangelist preachers
who sat it moral judgment of you
disguised in the lies as he teaches,
Crying, "Do as I say, not as I do."

Religious leaders aim to be all-knowing,
interpreting and memorizing every part.
If profits are showing, wealth keeps growing.
It's all a business led by atheists at heart.

Each one will tell their own story,
that the Lord is truly their friend.
Only they will rise in his glory,
while the others will perish in the end.

I have listened to all of your sermons.
I've seen the deeds that you've done.
I had looks at the books that determine
what makes you the chosen one.

I have seen your militant martyrs
and witnessed retaliation extreme,
all followed by political charters,
a perpetual cycle all too obscene.

In Mecca, find love and understanding.
Obedience brings a peaceful life.
Be careful not to be too demanding,
especially if you're somebody's wife.

One may say as you pray for a loved one,
"Please give a home to all the exiled,"
then decide, if it is a daughter or son,
to strap a bomb on the arm of the child.

Each one will tell their own story,
that the Lord is truly their friend.
Only they will rise in his glory,
while the others will perish in the end.

Judaism created the "one God" idea.
The concept was adopted by all.
Whether the end is distant or near,
all believe in the final roll call.

But you choose to dwell on your stories
and not to seek to find common ground.
You'd rather speak of defeats and of glories,
than discover a lasting peace collectively found.

All religion is based in tradition,
passed down from a long time ago,
steeped in fear, death, and superstition,
taught to all as things we must know.

Beware of the self-proclaimed enlightened
with the goal to control what you do.
Using confusing words devised for the frightened.
Never let others do your thinking for you.

Each one will tell their own story,
that the Lord is truly their friend.
Only they will rise in his glory,
while the others will perish in the end.

Postscript to Chapter 7

"The Fine Line" was written in 2017. Young minds can be fragile and easily swayed. They need to question what's being sold to them.

"Things We Were Taught to Believe," written in 2016, first was a poem. Then it became a song about the evolution of reality.

"Wake Up, Sunshine," written in 1971, is a song questioning where innocence has gone and how we are a product of your environment.

"Save Yourselves" is a poem written in 2010. I have found no matter where you travel on earth, beware of the self-proclaimed enlightened people. Always think for yourself, there are many who would like to do that for you. This poem was latter transformed into a song.

CHAPTER 8

Imagine a Deserted Beach

The three poems in this chapter relate to our desires. Whether dreaming of that unapproachable partner, a utopian society, or just to get away for a while, we should never stop dreaming.

- My Mirror Must Be Broken
- A Place We Only Dream Of
- I Need a Vacation

My Mirror Must Be Broken

Maybe she would notice me if I were a little taller.
Only a better-looking me would have the nerve to call her.
Perhaps if I lost some weight, she'd give me a second glance.
A stronger me might get a date, but she'd never want to dance.

If I were an alpha male, I'm sure she'd come a-calling.
Between my legs I'd take my tail; finally, I'd stop crawling.
But I am who I'm going to be. It's sad, but no jokin'.
If my reflection is the image of me, my mirror must be broken.

When I look at her, my heart starts pounding.
If she turned my way, what would she see?
If she listened to me, how would I be sounding?
She wouldn't care. What's wrong with me?

Now if I were a smarter man, I'd choose another way,
devise a precise and perfect plan with ideal words to say.
I've heard be honest with yourself, that the truth will set you free.
If I want to like someone else, first I must like me.

A Place We Only Dream Of

I went looking for a place
where people are kind,
in search of a land
so hard to find.

But in my pursuit
I found deep in each soul
an abundance of love that
even hating hearts hold.

So be gone with your bias.
What remains will be love.
And we'll all make this land
a place we only dream of.

I Need a Vacation

I need a vacation. I have to get away
from all the frustration of the day-to-day.
I need a vacation, the relaxing kind,
a one-way ticket to peace of mind.

So hard to keep the pace, maintain the speed.
Bumper cars in a rat race, jockeying for the lead.
Every day the same routine, seven thirty to four.
I need a change of scenery—can't take it anymore.

I need a vacation, a place where I can stay
until all my troubles just fade away.
I need a vacation, the soothing kind,
where peace and tranquility are all you find.

Like a boxer in a fight, a contender every day,
You want black or white, and all I see is gray.
Must have it immediately; don't keep me waiting.
I need to set my soul free; my strength is fading.

I need a vacation, an escape from this cell,
to a distant shoreline where I can sit a spell.
I need a vacation from this corporate climb,
where I can stand still and so can time.

Imagine a deserted beach, walking barefoot in the sand,
communication out of reach, meandering hand in hand,
a blue sky, a bright warn sun, a cool breeze in the air.
Relax, unwind, enjoy the fun—life without a care.

But now reality sets in, back on the fast track.
Whatever it takes to win, pedal to the metal, attack.
Now get out of my way, because I deserve the prize.
Struggling for the highest pay, can you hear the cries?

I need a vacation. I have to get away
from all the frustration of the day-to-day.
I need a vacation, the relaxing kind,
a one-way ticket to peace of mind.

Postscript to Chapter 8

"My Mirror Must Be Broken," written in 2004, is a song written about a very shy guy who is not I.

"A Place We Only Dream Of" is a poem I wrote in high school in 1968.

"I Need a Vacation" was a poem written in 2008. My wife came home from work one day and asked me to write a song; I needed a vacation, so I did.

CHAPTER 9

Afraid as I, and Wishes of We

Sometimes in our lives the world can seem overwhelming, and wishing for change seems fruitless. The three poems in this chapter express a yearning for things to get better. All were written over forty-five years ago, and the sentiments stand the test of time.

- Take a Moment (Just Listen)
- It All Seems So Futile
- We All Need a Little Love

Take a Moment (Just Listen)

If you listen, you can hear them cry.
Look closely, you will see them die.
Why must there be so much pain?
Some live in the path of the hurricane.

Take a moment for what it's worth.
Look at people anywhere on earth.
Then you will recognize for sure
the suffering others must endure.

A homeless family living in the street.
A missing child leaves an empty seat.
If these matters do not affect you.
There are more important things to do.

Why must the children cry?
How can we just let them die?
Does there have to be so much pain?
Some live in the path of the hurricane.

Why? Does it have to be this way?
Why? I try to discern.
Why? Day after day.
When will we ever learn?

In all the prisons, not an empty cell.
The sick are getting sicker; the rich do well.
See the sad face on the man in the moon?
A soldier writing home, "I'll be there soon."

A child not allowed beyond the gate.
A world filled with apathy and hate.
Civilians bombed in the name of God.
Why must their lives be so hard?

You may cover your ears so as not to hear the cry
of the hungry, starving, destined to die.
Hide your head in the sand so as not to see the pain
of the people in the path of the hurricane.

Why? Does it have to be this way?
Why? I try to discern.
Why? Day after day.
When will we ever learn?

Does it really take an earthquake
for your sleeping souls to awake?
Why do we need a tragedy
to have wide-open eyes see?

Take a moment for what it's worth
Look at people anywhere on earth.
Then you will begin to see
that how it is doesn't need to be.

If you listen, you can hear them cry.
Look closely, you will see them die.
Why must there be so much pain?
Life in the path of the hurricane.

It All Seems So Futile

My pillow is soaked with tears never cried.
My heart mourns for people who haven't died.
I pray to someone I don't even know.
It all seems so futile.

I look at the mirror, and the face is mine.
I can see the clock, but it tells only time.
I wake up to find just another day.
It all seems so futile.

I look at an adult and see only a child.
So many people who never smile.
As time goes on, every day is the same.
It all seems so futile.

I ask a question to which there is no answer.
I often wonder just what we're here for.
I look around to see that there'll never be peace.
It all seems so futile.

For minutes and hours to pass, I wait.
For destiny to determine my fate.
For the time I realize what is real.
It all seems so futile.

But time flows by like an endless stream.
My pillow in filled with dreams yet to dream.
Life isn't always as it may seem.
Futile thoughts are just futile.

We All Need a Little Love

An orphan child plays alone
and often dreams of a happy home.
Afraid as I and wishes of we,
his yearning desire is yet to be.

He just needs a helping hand
and to be with people who understand
and give him what he only dreams of.
All he needs is a little love.

A young mother is filled with fears,
attempting to suppress her tears.
She wishes her husband could hold her,
but his fate is as a distant soldier.

She could use a helping hand
and to be with people who understand.
His safe return she dreams of.
All she needs is a little love.

When you find someone feeling down,
lift them up; help them come around.
You'll feel good. It's the right thing to do.
Who knows, next time it may be you.

An old man stands beside a grave,
reminiscing of the life she gave.
His will to live on is now gone,
he knows not how he'll get along.

He just needs a helping hand
and to be with people who understand.
He needs to talk about what he dreams of.
All he needs is a little love.

At times, we all need a helping hand
And to be with people who understand.
We need to talk about what we dream of.
We all need a little love.

Postscript to Chapter 9

"Take a Moment (Just Listen)" a poem, written in 1967 when I was age fifteen. It was originally titled "Why Must a Baby Cry?"

"It All Seems So Futile," written in 1971, was originally a poem written by a good friend, Laura Kopf. I modified the words and turned it into a song.

"We All Need a Little Love" was written in 1973. If you help others, they will be there to help you when you need it.

CHAPTER 10

Never Expose Your Chin

This chapter contains three poems with very different moods. There are times when you may feel superstitious, and there are times when you want to conceal how you feel. But always remember that your response to any situation is solely determined by you.

- Two Digits (Triskaidekaphobia)
- If It Hurts
- Smile

Two Digits (Triskaidekaphobia)

What is it but a number,
two digits notwithstanding,
that causes such a commotion?

This problem I encumber
lacks logical understanding.
I need to contemplate the notion.

A one and a three, very simple to me,
not so different from others I hear.
Each is fine alone, but if together they're shown,
they cause such excitement and fear.

Now there are all kinds of theories of why this is,
and the explanations don't make any sense.
You may listen to hers and then listen to his
about a mere member in a numerical sequence.

The premise seems inexplicable
though the story goes on without fail.
How can a number be despicable?
The perpetuation of a tacit tall tale.

So, no need for trepidation.
Superstition is obscene.
You have an obligation.
Count on number thirteen.

If It Hurts

Let confidence be your style.
If love needs an inch, give a mile.
Serious decisions take a while.
If it hurts, just smile.

When given a whole, share half.
Fight the bull, not the calf.
Fish on the line, get the gaff.
If it hurts, just laugh.

In a battle, fight to win.
Never expose your chin.
Positive thoughts within.
If it hurts, just grin.

If the truth hurts, tell a lie.
When it's time to go, say goodbye.
And if a loved one should ever die,
If it hurts, just cry.

Smile

Life is brief,
a mere moment in time.

Enjoy the ups,
anticipate the decline.

Throughout the journey,
know the ordeal.

Every day,
you choose
how you feel.

Smile.

Postscript to Chapter 10

"Two Digits (Triskaidekaphobia)," written in 2006, is a poem that plays with rhyming patterns and the fear of the number 13.

"If It Hurts" was written in 2008. Don't show weakness in a fight, but if a loved one dies, then it's all right.

"Smile" was written in 2003. It is ultimately your call on how you feel. Don't let others bring you down.

CHAPTER 11

You Can't Be Wrong

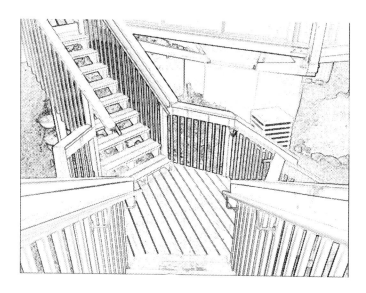

Have you ever noticed that the people who argue the most rarely listen? Even when they're are not talking, they're just thinking of what to say next. The three poems in this chapter address these types of individuals.

- Disagreements
- A Hollow Genius
- Negotiations

Disagreements

Disagreements can be settled when not left to linger,
expressing points of view without pointing a finger.

Speak your mind and then get out of the way
and truly listen to what the other has to say.

Resolving the issue should not be giving in,
while the goal should not be solely to win.

Finding common ground will always be wise
and can be attained when both compromise.

But do not debate with one who wants to vent.
They look not for answers but seek an argument.

A Hollow Genius

You're never happy with what you've got.
You always want what you have not.

When the sun is shining, you'd prefer rain.
And when it starts to pour, you complain.

You love to debate the opposing side.
If asked to commit, you run and hide.

You can't be wrong with results in hand.
As things deviate that others planned.

There isn't a risk with no skin in the game.
A hollow genius points a finger of blame.

Try making a decision, then proceed to act,
not critique the participants after the fact.

Make your opinion clear before the start,
So if it's not quite right, we can tear it apart.

And be there when new plans loom large.
You can feel what it's like to be in charge.

Negotiations

Doing the right thing is not always the right thing to do
when dealing with an enemy intent on destroying you.

If you deal with the devil, he will always agree,
until you turn your back and no longer can see.

He will pick your pocket and stab you in the back,
Then wait for the right time to carry out an attack.

Your dialogue and handshake were perceived as weak.
For the rupture of the dam starts with just a little leak.

You need to come out swinging while carrying a big stick,
So they hear you loud and clear and get the message quick.

To trust this type of opponent is a decision made by fools.
You will lose if you're the only side that plays by the rules.

Always be prepared by being ready, willing, and able,
Knowing that battles are lost at the negotiation table.

But never stop communicating, and keep peace in sight.
The pen is mightier than the sword if you're ready to fight.

Postscript to Chapter 11

"Disagreements," written in 2014, is a poem expressing a good way to settle arguments, listen, and compromise.

"A Hollow Genius" was written in 2010. A Monday morning quarterback can't be wrong.

"Negotiations" was written in 2015. The pen is mightier than the sword when you're carrying a big stick.

CHAPTER 12

Our Coincidence of Meeting

This chapter contains three poems that are also love songs that tend to sound better as lyrics. The lyrics speak to the timing of love. The first poem starts with love early in life; the second, love later in life; and the third, love that is completely out of sync.

- I Want to Be There
- Never Needed Anyone
- How Many Times?

I Want to Be There

I recall the first time
I saw you standing there,
the stars in your eyes,
the moonlight on your hair.
A prettier picture could never be,
now frozen in time,
only my mind's eye can see.
The planets aligned,
everything felt right.
Could it really be
love at first sight?

When you wake up in the morning,
I want to be there, be the one to care for you.
You won't be alone. In a home of our own,
we'll take on the world as two.

When people meet for
the very first time,
they find it hard to express
what's on their minds.
Simple words become
difficult to say,
allowing nervous thoughts
to get in the way.
At the inception,
I forgot my name.
I knew right then
that life would never be the same.

When you wake up in the morning,
I want to be there, be the one to care for you.
You won't be alone. In a home of our own,
we'll take on the world as two.

Time flies by at such a fast pace.
It's tough to have much to show.
But I still see a smile on your face
as you ask, "Where did the time go?"

Now we have been together
for so many years,
through the joy of laughter,
the sorrow, and tears,
as friends and lovers,
husband and wife,
companions forever
throughout our life.
From the beginning
it was plain to see,
our coincidence of meeting
was meant to be.

When you wake up in the morning,
I want to be there, be the one to care for you.
You won't be alone. In a home of our own,
we'll take on the world as two.

Never Needed Anyone

I never needed anyone until you came along.
You touched my soul. You made me whole.
I never needed anyone.

I was surprised to find someone like you
whom I could hold. My dreams to you I told.
I was surprised to find.

You make me feel alive. Now that you're in my life,
I have so much thanks to your touch,
You make me feel alive.

I was content with life as it was,
just living from day to day,
happy with the path that I was on.
But you came and changed my way.

I never needed anyone until you came along.
You touched my soul. You made me whole.
I never needed anyone.

How Many Times?

How many times did I tell you I love you,
and how many times did I show you I care?
Seeing as now I don't know if I still do,
finally you want me. Now I doubt you.

I remember times when we were together.
Hours at a time, we would hold one another.
As a friend and a lover, and who was who,
recalling a very good day or maybe two.

Some couples grow closer together,
while others drift farther apart.
It would have been better to know one another
than what we thought at the start.

How many times did I give you my love?
And wasn't I always a gentleman to you?
Now I hear that for our love you were blind.
You want me now; you changed your mind.

Well, you made me feel weak when I wanted to look strong.
When I said we were meant to be, you
laughed and said I was wrong.
But now as I begin to think back again,
I will recall you as just an old friend.

How many times did I tell you I love you,
and how many times did I show you I care?
Because now I don't know if I really do.
Finally you want me. I've found someone new.

Postscript to Chapter 12

"I Want to Be There" written in 1972, was first a song written for Janet that I slightly modified for Valentine's Day 2013.

"Never Needed Anyone" was written in 2008. It was first a song I composed in fifteen minutes, lyrics and music both.

"How Many Times?" written in 1971, is a song describing a situation where a couple's love, musically speaking, was out of time.

CHAPTER 13

Alleviate the Pain

This chapter contains three poems that address the sadness and the obstacles some must encounter in their struggle to be free.

- Ode to a Friend
- Someday Soon
- Chasing That Elusive Ghost

Ode to a Friend

Through the flames I see a vision,
a struggle, not entirely clear.
Two figures are fighting,
which suddenly arouses my fear.
As I peer a bit closer
from beyond, I see it must be a sign.
I come to the realization
that the two faces are mine.

An arm extended above the head
clutching a spike-like knife.
Down forth comes the blow,
in an attempt to take my life.
A loud scream is then released,
for then there is no sound.
The image starts to fade away,
and slowly I come down.

Someday Soon

I am feeling so depressed, I think I'm going mad.
Each new day becomes the worst I've ever had.
When will it ever change? Can it be a curse?
Future expectations seem to be getting worse.

Someday soon the sun will show through.
Someday soon it will shine on me too.
Someday soon is not so far away.
Someday soon is going to be my day.

I feel that life has dealt me a losing hand.
I think that I have taken all that I can stand.
I wonder if there is an eventual end in sight.
I want to throw in the towel, give up the fight.

Someday soon the sun will show through.
Someday soon it will shine on me too.
Someday soon seems so far away.
Someday soon—I can't take another day.

Now time has passed; it is over. This is what I found.
The lower you go, the higher you'll rebound.
And it has been this way since the human race has been run.
If you hang on just a little more, you'll bask in the sun.

Chasing That Elusive Ghost

It all started with a minor sports injury,
something to alleviate the pain.
Although it was targeted for the muscles,
something was erupting in the brain.

Eventually, the soreness subsided.
Potentially seemed better than before.
Wanting never to endure that again
but desiring the remedy even more.

Sooner or later the medicine ran out,
so you quietly solicited around.
It didn't take too much time.
A substitute was easily found.

Decided to withdraw from sports,
and school was "no longer for me."
Really didn't need them anymore,
wanted everyone to "just let me be."

But soon cost spiraled out of control.
You had to beg, borrow, and steal.
Couldn't care less who you hurt,
for nothing in life seemed real.

Popping pills rapidly became blasé
and ultimately lost its charm.
In search of the highest high,
you hit rock bottom, a needle in the arm.

But for a moment it was total bliss,
no recall of who, where, or when.
Pursue it for the rest of your life;
you'll never feel that way again.

So continue on your merry way
while chasing that elusive ghost.
It's like grabbing a handful of smoke.
The drug's the parasite; you're the host.

We all know how these stories end.
Oftentimes it is not very good.
Getting caught in the revolving rehab,
overdosing, and a box of wood.

It all goes back to the beginning,
a patient's comfort, a goal to attain.
A doctor gets credit for the healing.
Know in time that nature relieves the pain.

Postscript to Chapter 13

"Ode to a Friend," written in 1970, is about a mural painted on a friend's wall.

"Someday Soon" was written in 1969 as a song for a childhood friend with a debilitating illness.

"Chasing That Elusive Ghost" a poem written in 2017. Endure the pain. It may be better than the parasitic alternatives.

CHAPTER 14

For Better or for Worse

This chapter addresses three distinct levels of scrutiny. The first is an intimate curiosity of how a long-lost friend has made out in life. The second questions the fundamental relationship between war and religion. The last tackles the so-called sanctity of marriage.

- I Wonder about Her
- Now and Forevermore
- A Confusion Delusion (Divorce, of Course)

I Wonder about Her

I remember her hair, so lovely and long.
I recall the way she'd smile when I'd sing her a song.
I'd see her eyes light up as if the sun
were beaming warmth and love, her gift to everyone.
Sometimes I wonder where she is today,
how I let someone like that get away.
But no matter where she is, I hope that she's happy.
Sometimes I just wonder if she thinks about me.
Because at times I find that I wonder about her.

I remember her voice, so soft, so mild.
She always carried herself with incredible style.
Arms always open, she had a gentle touch.
She gave all she had and felt it was never enough.
But I contemplate from time to time
how she looks today, what's on her mind.
Does she possess a world of wealth, or is she trapped in poverty?
Sometimes I just wonder if she thinks about me.
Because at times I find that I wonder about her.

I remember her laugh. It would warm my heart.
Oh, how alone I felt whenever we were apart.
What a sense of humor. She and I could laugh all night.
I remember making a vow never to let her out of my sight.
But sometimes feelings change deep within one's soul.
Time speeds incredibly fast, seemingly out of control.
Now I wish her life to be the best that it can be.
Sometimes I just wonder if she thinks about me.
Because at times I find that I wonder about her.

Now and Forevermore

On the shores of a lavish land, humanity prepares to sin.
Where an abandoned lighthouse stands, a war is about to begin.
The waters are rough and the tide rolls
out—no time to say goodbye.
The ships are being tossed about; you can see their flags fly.

The battle started at the break of day. A dozen men fell.
"Come back, come back! Please stay," you can hear a mother yell.
The fort stands along the sea; the cannons explode like thunder.
The people rejoice: "We're free! We're
free!" Another ship goes under.

Dark clouds blow in from the rear, completely covering the sky.
The sunlight wants to disappear, but the flags continue to fly.
Rapidly a dense fog billows in, cloaking the sea and the land.
Opposing enemies, intending to win, take their gallant stand.

Fighting foes, they can barely see, and why they begin to analyze.
"I pray the next one won't be me." The death toll continues to rise.
But alas, now something arises. You can see a single sunray.
A strong wind begins to blow and takes the smoke and fog away.

Now one can see mass devastation as one scans from left to right.
The last form of communication, a faint cry, "Get up and fight."
An observer on a distant hill feels he knows not and never will.
And we are destined to stay that way
until we gain comprehension of
"Thou shall not kill."

A Confusion Delusion (Divorce, of Course)

As you're walking, talking, heading for the door,
You're in conversation, imagination, laying down your law.
I was ordered, defrauded, nearly left for dead.
I was framed, defamed, guilty. "Off with his head!"
You were refusing, accusing, conjuring up a tale.
You were defying, again lying, fighting tooth and nail.

A confusion delusion, that's all it really is.
Bonds of vows breaking, dividing hers and his.
A confusion delusion; you cannot make amends.
A mushroom cloud scenario, that's how it always ends.

The odds are stacked against you when you tie the knot.
The grass is always greener; you want what you have not.
So, when you said for better or for worse, it all was just a lie.
For when love turns to a state of hate, it is time to say goodbye.

But I rejected, deflected, refused to take the fall.
Shared blame, overcame, proudly standing tall.
You're needing, repeating; you've said it all before.
Your diction is all fiction. I listen to you no more.
Time to move on, be gone. Karma takes and gives.
I decree, as a visionary, she had ulterior motives.

A confusion delusion, changing what was to what is.
Individualities drift away, distancing hers and his.
A confusion delusion, another matrimonial loss.
Their pledge, over the edge, ends of course in divorce.

Postscript to Chapter 14

"I Wonder about Her," written in 1972, is a song revisited later with multiple individuals in mind.

"Now and Forevermore," written in 1969 when I was seventeen years old, is a critique of war and religion.

"A Confusion Delusion (Divorce, of Course)" was written in 2017. I had no one in mind when I wrote it, but the rhymes just kept coming.

CHAPTER 15

Nothing Forever Survives

The four poems in this chapter attempt to set a path to a virtuous and fulfilled life, focusing on behavior, accomplishment, reflection, and happiness.

- Life in a Nutshell
- Success
- Life's Too Short
- The Ultimate Goal

Life in a Nutshell

From a cry to a sigh, life begins and ends.
The first breath, the last moan, again and again.
We listen, we think, we interpret, we say.
And the progression continues day after day.

Each one in line must take their turn,
pass the baton, teach what they've learned.
Like dominos standing, eventually to fall,
fates that awaits each one and all.

But when you go, you're not really gone.
Your words and actions echo on and on.
So, what you speak and how you behave
has infinite possibilities from cradle to grave.

Success

Accolades are in the shallows;
achievement is in the deep.
Happiness is contingent upon
the company that you keep.
For time waits for no one,
and nothing forever survives.
Enjoy each moment together,
traversing each other's lives.

Life's Too Short

I haven't cried since my mother died.
Twenty years have flown by.
Why that's so, I don't know.
I couldn't tell you why.

It was sad when I lost my dad
early in the past year.
And in the end, when I lost my friend,
I couldn't shed a tear.

I know they're gone. Life goes on,
but I miss them every day.
If I'd had a chance or knew in advance,
I wonder what they'd say.

All I know is that not so long ago,
life was filled with family and friends.
But in time, no reason or rhyme,
their days with us just ended.

With this thought, life's too short,
don't let trivial things get in the way.
Be sure it shows. Let loved ones know
that you appreciate them every day.

It won't be long before your own swan song
will play as your final sun sets.
But keep in mind that what you leave behind
should be a life without any regrets.

The Ultimate Goal

You may choose to take it easy or select to seize it swift,
knowing that time is of the essence and life is but a gift.

If you exercise and watch your diet, results can be synthetic.
Good health is what we wish for, though basically it's genetic.

Make it clear, it is here. You will ignite your fire.
Don't let fear commandeer your heart's desire.

Seek knowledge, finish college, train your brain.
Satisfaction is the attraction. No pain, no gain.

Keep your family and friends not too far away.
Include a scheduled recess and play every day.

And, of course, at a loss, grief may be a reaction.
Keep in sight what is right. Sustain good traction.

Treat everyone fair, and then you'll have no bridges to burn.
In time, you'll find you're treated kind in turn.

And after all is said and done,
the ultimate goal is to have fun.
Listen here, everyone:

laughter is what you're after.

Postscript to Chapter 15

"Life in a Nutshell," written in 2002, is a poem I turned into a song, my personal favorite.

"Success," written in 2016, is a passage to be deciphered for its content.

"Life's Too Short," written in 2015, expresses that idea that a life without regrets is as good as it gets.

"The Ultimate Goal" was written in 2015. Have fun, enjoy every day, and keep laughing.

CHAPTER 16

One Question

As I opened the first chapter of this book with only one entry, I will do the same with this final chapter. This book has given you my opinion on many topics over a fifty-year span. Although there may be some serious issues addressed herein, I believe that the overall theme of *One's Perspective* is to live life to the fullest, keep a positive attitude, and laugh as much as you can. So, I will end with a poem I wrote over fifty years ago that alludes to the mystery of life and maybe the reason why I have written every poem since.

- Final Thoughts (Life's Conundrum)

Final Thoughts (Life's Conundrum)

I, like the lone lamb
lost from the flock,
find myself face-
to-face with the clock.

Now knowing my time
has flown by too fast,
I realize my future
is reliving my past.

And as we all must
inevitably say goodbye,
I have but one question:
why?

Postscript to Chapter 16

"Final Thoughts (Life's Conundrum)," written in 1968 when I was fifteen years old. Was originally titled "Thoughts of an Old Man."

Closing Words

Soon you will be nothing more than a memory, so make your life something worth remembering.

Printed in the United States
By Bookmasters